I AM

The Self Guide To Your Success

Yolanda Anderson

True Vine Media

Unless otherwise indicated, all Scripture
quotations are taken from the King James
Version of the Bible.
Scripture quotations marked (AMPC) are taken
from The Amplified Bible, Classic Edition
Copyright © 1954, 1958, 1962, 1964, 1965, 1987
by The Lockman Foundation

Scripture quotations marked NLT are taken
from the Holy Bible, New Living Translation,
Copyright © 1996, 2004, 2015 by Tyndale House
Foundation. Used by permission of Tyndale
House Publishers, Inc., Carol Stream, Illinois

60188.

Britannica, The Editors of Encyclopedia. "Yahweh". Encyclopedia Britannica, 30 Jun. 2021, https://www.britannica.com/topic/Yahweh. Accessed 3 December 2021.

Merriam-Webster.com. 2021. https://www.merriam-webster.com (3 December 2021).

Anderson, Y. (2021, December 3). Yahweh. Wikipedia. Retrieved December 3, 2021, from https://www.wikipedia.org/

Printed in the United States of America
First Edition

This Book is Dedicated to

GOD

The

GREAT I AM

"God cannot lie, and He is The Spirit of Truth. Whatever He says, it is so. The work concerning us is already done. This gives us the confidence (faith) to operate as His offspring. We can be who we decree to be because He is who He decrees to be. Jeshua is the embodiment and fulfillment of "I Am" – John 1:14"

DR. TODD J. PULLIAM

INTRODUCTION

The power to succeed already lies within you. In this book you will explore how "death and life are in the power of your tongue" (Proverbs 18:21). The purpose of this book is to enable you to start thinking and to go in the direction of positive thoughts and confessions about your life; to know the power that lies within you! Take your wings and soar to the top with the powerful insight of "I AM".

PREFACE

Beloved,

We have the responsibility to live in the promises of God. He left them to us to exemplify that WE are HIS OWN in the earth. You may ask, how do I live the good of the Word, when life throws me circumstances that prevent me from doing so? He left us His Name! He left us His Power. He left us HIS AUTHORITY.

PART 1

◆ ◆ ◆

WHAT IS HIS NAME?

Based on Britannica, God's Name—YHWH (Yahweh), the God of the Israelites, means, most properly – "He Brings into Existence whatever Exist"

He told Moses, when asked, "You shall Say Unto the Children of Israel, I AM hath sent you (Exodus 3:14)

"I AM", consists of His Control. We see listed in the scriptures several times where God referred to Himself as "I AM". And thus, when Yahweh, the Creator of the Universe declares Himself to Be "I AM that I AM" in Exodus 3:14, He is ultimately allowing us to see His Power. Notice that I called Yahweh–GOD, The Creator of the Universe. We often make that sound mystical–like WOW! In no way am I taking away From GOD and His Power, but, let's look at that in its simplest meaning.

Webster defines Creator as one that creates, usually by bringing something new or original into being. Another defines it as a person or thing that brings something into existence.

As we see here, a creator is one who

causes something to be that was not originally. Genesis chapter 1 shows us this:

In the Beginning, God Created the Heaven, and the Earth. And the Earth was WITHOUT FORM and VOID and DARKNESS was upon the FACE of the Deep. And the Spirit of God moved upon the face of the waters. And GOD SAID, Let There BE LIGHT and THERE WAS Light. And GOD SAID, LET THERE BE a firmament in the midst of the waters, and let it divide the waters from the waters. And GOD MADE the firmament and divided the waters which were under the firmament from the waters which were above the firmament and IT WAS SO. (Genesis 1:1-3; 6-7)

We see the Original Creation, where God took completely empty (void) and not valid darkness and began to make a masterpiece. How could He do this? Let's go back to HOW He defines Himself–His Name.

The Hebrew phrase: יהוה was English translated as "I Am that I Am;" it also translates as, "I will Become what I choose to Become;" or "I will Be what I will Be," and even "I Create What(ever) I Create."

Know that God in all His Power, Is who He Is, and *Creates* whatever He chooses to *Create*.

> *And God Said, Let Us make MAN in Our IMAGE and AFTER Our LIKENESS and let them have dominion over the fish of the sea, over the fowl of the air, and over the cattle, and over all the earth, and over every creeping thing that*

creepeth upon the earth (27) So God CREATED Man in HIS OWN IMAGE, in the IMAGE of GOD created He him; male and female created He them. (28) And God Blessed them, and GOD SAID unto them, BE fruitful and multiply and REPLENISH the earth and subdue it; and have DOMINION over the fish of the sea, and over the fowl of the air, and over every living thing that moveth upon the earth. (Genesis 1: 26-28)

I love breaking things into their simplest forms, so let's define some terms.

Dominion: sovereignty or control; (Sovereignty: supreme power or authority.)

Image: 1) a representation of a person or thing in art; 2) a person or thing that closely resembles another; 3) semblance or likeness. (Semblance: the outward appearance or apparent form of something, especially when the reality is different).

These terms help us understand the verses better. We clearly see that when God created man, He made him as a closely resembling representation of Himself. We also realized more certainly that He gave man SUPREME power or authority–NOT OVER EACH OTHER–but over all that was created in the Earth. How cool is that?

PART 2

• • •

HOW DOES "I AM" WORK FOR YOU?

By Faith [that is, with an inherent trust and enduring confidence in the power, wisdom and goodness of God] we understand that the worlds (Universe, ages) were framed and created [formed put in order and equipped for their intended purpose] by the WORD of God, so that what is seen was NOT MADE out of things which are visible. (Hebrews 11:3 AMPC)

In part one of this guide, we found out Yahweh's Hebrew name translated into I AM that I AM or, more relevantly, I Create What(ever) I Create, exemplifying His GREAT Authority. So, how does "I AM" work for you? Let's explore more of *who* man *IS*.

When I consider thy heavens, the work of thy fingers, the moon and the stars, which thou hast ordained: What is man, that thou art mindful of him? And the son of man, that thou visitest him? For thou hast made him a little lower than the angels and has crowned him with glory and honour. Thou madest him to have dominion over the works of thy hands; thou hast put all things under his feet (Psalms 8: 3-6)

The writer (David) questions the creator, in awe of His affectionate connection to man (the creation), that He would give him *supreme control* over everything else HE made. We go back to Genesis, where we know it all began. God told the Godhead, Let's make man like US!

Babies, of any species are 'LIKE 'their parents. They look like, act like and even have the same character traits as their parent. They may not be the exact same in everything, but most of what is in the parent is in the child. When God SAID, "Let Us make man like Us", He was suggesting that His character traits be input into man. This is why He is referred to as our Father. We know that God is the *all-powerful* Creator. How does this filter into us?

The Spirit itself beareth witness with our spirit that we are the children of God (Romans 8:16)

The most powerful tool we have to validate us as God's children is His Spirit on the inside of us. We now know, once we've accepted Christ as our Lord and Savior and His ways, we are equipped with the same power and sovereignty as our Father. We are ranked after His order. Meaning He has His ruling, and He has given us that which we are to rule over *("The heaven, even the heavens, are the LORD'S: but the earth hath he given to the children of men."* Psalm 115:16) – but yet, WE ARE TO RULE. Hebrews 11:3 told us that by faith (God's Faith in what HE would say would *be)* the Earth was made. Being made in His likeness, we too should have that *same faith.*

2 Corinthians 4: 13 – We, having the

SAME spirit of Faith, according as it is written, I Believed, and therefore have I spoken, we also Believe and THEREFORE SPEAK!

THIS is how "I AM" is to work for us. We are to BELIEVE and then SPEAK. As we once again go back to Genesis–where it/ we ALL began, we recognize that when God, THE CREATOR, made the Universe – HE SPOKE! The Power of Who HE IS— YHWH – "I AM That I AM"—is a creative force, thus whatever "I AM" SPOKE – had TO BE or manifest, simply because HE SAID IT!

Let's look again at the notion that what's in the parent is in the child. Based on the verses, once we accept Christ as our Lord, we are then CHILDREN of The Most High GOD. Since GOD–YHWH–I AM is our FATHER, as a child, we too are God.

"I have said, Ye are gods; and ALL

of you are children of the Most HIGH!" (Psalms 82:5) (also John 10:34 as a NT reference).

HE GAVE US HIS NAME!!

In our society, when you have a certain "last name", you are thought to have a particular power or prestige. It's like a *title of privilege.* We all know some "power" names in the world today. However, none of the names you can think of, will ever compare to the one we, as believers, were given – "I AM"! *We* have even greater *privileges* with the use of His Name as *His* children; It is our GOD-GIVEN right.

Since we KNOW we have rights, let's walk in them! What person, knowing that they have wealth and power, wouldn't use it to their full advantage? That is like walking around as if you are poor or broke, with millions in the bank. Almost NO ONE would do that, right? "I AM" is your name of power and prestige to use to your advantage. It holds *CREATIVE* power. Use of it, allows you to change your world.

PART 3

◆ ◆ ◆

"I AM"

Recognizing your sonship is the first step. Once you realize you are the son of the Creator, it is then that you understand *you* too, have creative power within. We were given the most powerful name, and the Universe already knows how to respond to it.

And Moses said to God, Behold, when I come to the Israelites and say to them, The God of your fathers has sent me to you, and they say to me, What is His name? What shall I say to them? And God said to Moses, I Am Who I Am and What I Am, and I Will Be What I Will Be; and He said, You shall say this to the Israelites: I Am has sent me to you! (Exodus 3:13-14 AMPC)

Now let's take a look at verse 15

God said also to Moses, "THIS shall you say to the Israelites the LORD, the God of your Fathers of Abraham, of Isaac, and of Jacob, has sent me to you! THIS is My NAME FOREVER, and by THIS NAME I AM to be remembered to ALL Generations." (Exodus 3:15 AMPC)

LORD (Adonai), has been substituted for YHWH, as they are often parallel along with Jehovah. (Wikipedia)

Here we see God told Moses His Name; then He told him, let the people know My title is to be memorialized and used or passed down from generation to generation, FOREVER. To memorialize means to remember or preserve in memory. We are to REMEMBER *Who We Are* and *Where We Come From.* Our very existence started with God, the Creator, and we are His CHILDREN, therefore WE are CREATORS.

PART 4

◆ ◆ ◆

HOW TO USE
THE NAME

As stated earlier, the Universe was designed to recognize its Creator. When we, with *faith* and *authority*, *speak the name*: "I AM", the Universe "perks up" to work.

Genesis 1:3—And God (I AM) SAID, Let there BE Light; and there was Light.

The *POWER* is in GOD, so He didn't have to say, 'In My Name' BE and then it happened. NO–HE IS the *source* of power. but *we*, being grafted into that power, must use HIS Name like a badge to identify who we represent. So, when we, IN FAITH, speak confidently knowing the POWER that lies in that Name, we then also know the Universe perks up to work for us as well.

Soldiers are taught to follow a command–anyone coming with a command in the name (as a representative) of that individual's superior, causes that soldier to do as commanded. "I AM" is that *BADGE!* ANYTHING that follows it MUST manifest itself just *as if* Christ said it,

HIMSELF!

Matthew 12:37 KJV/NLT—KJV–"For by thy words thou shalt be justified, and by thy words thou shalt be condemned."   NLT–"The words you say will either acquit you or condemn you."

Mark 11:23d —"... he shall have whatsoever he saith"

*TH on the end of a word based on the Greek explanation, means habit. Therefore, SAITH means making it a habit to say

Scripture confirms again and again what God indicated from the Beginning... *You* can have WHATEVER you say in Faith (with an undeniable passion behind it). Utilizing "I AM", gets the power backing of the Universe to work for you. So, when you say, "I AM_____", good or bad, spoken with strong conviction... it's on its WAY! Everything aligns itself to get THAT very thing to you. Knowing this, make it work for your benefit.

Disclaimer: The God of the Universe will NOT let you use His Name to harm others.

The purpose of this book is to get you to start thinking; to go in the direction of positive thoughts about your life and to know the power that lies within you.

EPILOGUE

I have composed a starter list for you that will help you turn your life into the one you desire. We all understand, before you can utilize a name, you must first have that name. It's just like getting married or adopted. The name is given to you once you are a part of that family. The first thing I would like to offer you is to become a part of THE FAMILY!!!

If you are ready to get access to this Name, simply repeat this prayer

Lord Jesus, I recognize now, that You left a name for me that I have not understood the power of. I want to become a part of Your Family. Forgive me of my sins; be my Father

by coming into my heart and helping me walk in Your footsteps. I accept You now, as my Lord and Savior. Thank You for coming into my heart, saving me, making me completely new, and making me a part of Your royal family. Thank You for also allowing me to understand and know that I Am Your Child and now have every privilege of the use of Your name. Amen.

NOW, that you are IN, it does NOT take years, blood, sweat and tears to get where you want to be. It takes *faith*, commitment, and speech.

Take this list and complete it with those ideas, goals and dreams you desire to see in your life, and SPEAK them EVERY DAY. It works for me, so it will work for you! Much success is in your speech.

I AM

I AM Saved

I AM Forgiven

I AM Victory

I AM Healed

I AM Employment

I AM New Home

I AM Prospering in my Finances

I AM Reparations

I AM Free from Bondages

I AM Confidence

I AM Wisdom

I AM Peace of Mind

I AM Free of Debt

I AM Pretty

I AM Attracting Positivity

I AM Weight Loss

I AM Alert

I AM Without Lack

I AM Promotion

I AM Whole

I AM Good Health

I AM Long Life

I AM ENOUGH

Here is where YOU pick up. The pages following are for you to CREATE YOUR SUCCESS by writing your own I AM statements. Continue to add to and speak them daily. You WILL begin to see a change take place in your life. Happy Creating—God Bless!

I AM...

I AM...

I AM...

I AM...

I AM...

I AM...

ABOUT THE AUTHOR

Yolanda Anderson

A fourth-generation Believer who understands we have God-given rights afforded us from the Kingdom of Heaven that go unused. These rights and privileges and an understanding of how to use them would empower many Believers to live their best life. An educator, in her own right, Yolanda is a mother of two high school scholars. They all work together to educate as many Believers as possible, young and old, on how to walk in and live the best life God has to offer.